Editor
Janet Cain, M. Ed.

Editorial Project Manager
Ina Massler Levin, M.A.

Editor-in-Chief
Sharon Coan, M.S. Ed.

Illustrator
Bruce Hedges

Cover Artist
Denise Bauer

Art Coordinator
Kevin Barnes

Imaging
Ralph Olmedo, Jr.

Product Manager
Phil Garcia

Publisher
Mary D. Smith, M.S. Ed.

SPORTS BRAIN TEASERS

Grades 4 & Up

Author

Cynthia Holzschuher, M.S. Ed.

Teacher Created Resources

Teacher Created Resources, Inc.
6421 Industry Way
Westminster, CA 92683
www.teachercreated.com

ISBN: 978-0-7439-3352-0

©2002 Teacher Created Resource.
Reprinted, 2010
Made in U.S.A.

D1299687

Table of Contents

Introduction

Sports Brain Teasers provides ways to exercise and develop brain power! The popular sports topics will raise the interest level of even the most reluctant learner. Each page stands alone and can be used as a quick and easy filler activity. The pages can be distributed to individual students or used effectively with an entire class. These activities are especially useful in helping students develop the following:

- logic and critical-thinking skills
- creative-thinking skills
- research skills
- spelling skills
- general vocabulary and knowledge.

Nicknames Past and Present

Match the real names from the word bank with these baseball players' nicknames. Use the position each player played to help you with your answers.

1. The Georgia Peach (outfielder) _____

2. The Yankee Clipper (outfielder) _____

3. The Iron Horse (first baseman) _____

4. Mr. October (outfielder) _____

5. The Say Hey Kid (centerfielder) _____

6. Charlie Hustle (first, second, and third baseman; outfielder) _____

7. The Sultan of Swat (outfielder) _____

8. Hammerin' Hank (outfielder) _____

9. The Rocket (pitcher) _____

10. Shoeless (outfielder) _____

11. Catfish (pitcher) _____

12. Mr. Cub (shortstop) _____

13. The Big Hurt (first baseman) _____

14. Junior (centerfielder) _____

15. Iron Man (shortstop; third baseman) _____

Name Bank

Henry Aaron	Lou Gehrig	Willie Mays
Ernie Banks	Ken Griffey, Jr.	Cal Ripken, Jr.
Roger Clemens	Jim Hunter	Pete Rose
Ty Cobb	Joe Jackson	Babe Ruth
Joe DiMaggio	Reggie Jackson	Frank Thomas

Baseball Equations

Each equation below contains the first letters of words that will make it complete and explain how the number relates to baseball. Write the missing words. The first one has been done for you.

1. **9** = the number of _____**Players**_____ on a _____**Baseball Team**_____

2. **90** = the number of **F** _____ between **B** _____

3. **3** = the number of **S** _____ that make an **O** _____

4. **0** = the number of **H** _____ in a **N** _____ **H** _____

5. **9** = the number of **I** _____ in a **G** _____

6. **4** = the number of **R** _____ for a **G** _____ **S** _____

7. **4** = the number of **B** _____ **P** _____ on a **D** _____

8. **7** = the number of **G** _____ in the **W** _____ **S** _____

9. **14** = the number of **T** _____ in the **A** _____ **L** _____

10. **16** = the number of **T** _____ in the **N** _____ **L** _____

11. **5** = the number of **S** _____ on **H** _____ **P** _____

12. **4** = the number of **B** _____ that make a **W** _____

13. **5** ounces = the **W** _____ of a **B** _____

14. **4** = the number of **U** _____ per **G** _____

15. **1** = the number of **M** _____ per **T** _____

Links to Baseball Terminology

Fill in the blanks with new words that you create by changing one letter at a time, until you have changed each of the first words into the last words. An example has been done for you.

Example: ball _____bale_____ _____gale_____ **game**

1. minor _____ major

2. run _____ _____ hit

3. win _____ _____ bat

4. team _____ year

5. play _____ _____ slam

6. pitch _____ catch

7. home _____ _____ lost

8. foul _____ _____ _____ _____ beat

9. fair _____ _____ rain

10. save _____ _____ _____ lose

11. game _____ _____ base

12. bat _____ _____ _____ fly

Baseball Brothers

Read the clues. Then write the last names of these brothers and teammates.

1. **Milwaukee Braves (1962–1965)**

   Hank and Tommie A ____ ____ ____ ____

2. **San Francisco Giants (1963)**

   Matty, Felipe, and Jesus A ____ ____ ___

3. **Cincinnati Reds (1997–1998)**

   Bret and Aaron B ____ ____ ____ ____

4. **Oakland Athletics (1990)**

   Ozzie and Jose C ____ ____ ____ ____ ____ ____

5. **Oakland Athletics (2000–2001)**

   Jason and Jeremy G ____ ____ ____ ____ ____

6. **Montreal Expos (1998–2000)**

   Vladimir and Wilton G ____ ____ ____ ____ ____ ____ ____

7. **San Diego Padres (1996)**

   Chris and Tony G ____ ____ ____ ____

8. **Cincinnati Reds (1998)**

   Barry and Stephen L ____ ____ ____ ____ ____

9. **Los Angeles Dodgers (1992–1993), Boston Red Sox (1999–2001)**

   Pedro and Ramon M ____ ____ ____ ____ ____ ____ ____

10. **Atlanta Braves (1973–1974)**

    Joe and Phil N ____ ____ ____ ____ ____

11. **Baltimore Orioles (1987–1992, 1996)**

    Billy and Cal R ____ ____ ____ ____ ____

12. **Los Angeles Dodgers (1959–1962)**

    Larry and Norm S ____ ____ ____ ____ ____

Calling All Fans

Use the clues to name these major league baseball teams. An example has been provided for you.

Example: Minnesota identical pairs → Minnesota Twins

1. Baltimore yellow and black birds → Baltimore _____

2. New York Northerners → New York _____

3. Cleveland Native Americans → Cleveland _____

4. Detroit large, striped cats → Detroit _____

5. Kansas City ruling monarchs → Kansas City _____

6. Anaheim heavenly beings → Anaheim _____

7. Seattle seafarers → Seattle _____

8. Texas park service workers → Texas _____

9. Atlanta Indian warriors → Atlanta _____

10. Florida sailfish → Florida _____

11. Chicago young bears → Chicago _____

12. Pittsburgh buccaneers → Pittsburgh _____

13. St. Louis red birds → St. Louis _____

14. San Diego Spanish fathers → San Diego _____

15. San Francisco imaginary big people → San Francisco _____

Baseball's Triple Crown

For the baseball seasons indicated on the puzzle, fill in the names of the baseball players who have led their leagues in batting average, home runs, and runs batted all in the same season. Then arrange the circled letters to name the 1967 Triple Crown winner.

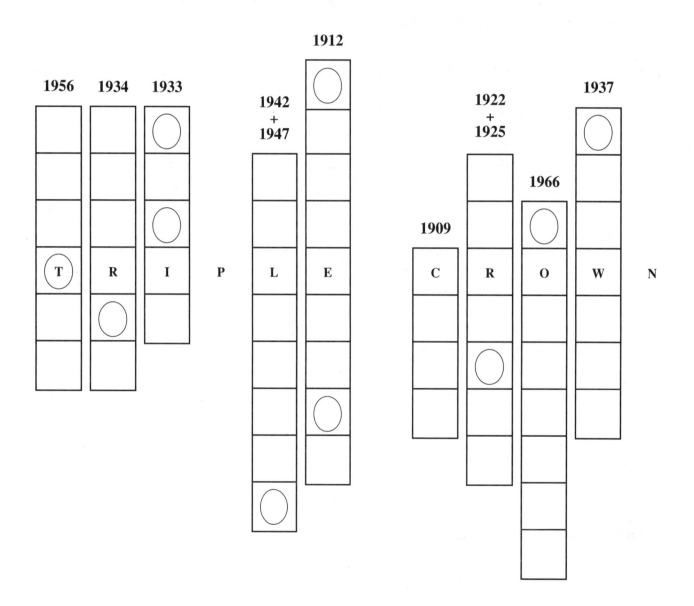

Bonus: Carl Y ____ ____ ____ ____ ____ ____ ____ ____ ____ ____ is the player who won the Triple Crown in 1967.

The "Streak"

Lou Gehrig and Cal Ripken, Jr., were consistent hitters and fielders. Each man ignored injury and illness to play in consecutive games for many years. Each played his entire career for only one team. There are many other similarities. However, there are also differences that make each player unique. For each statement, write an **X** in the appropriate column to indicate whether it describes Gehrig or Ripken, Jr.

Achievements	Gehrig	Ripken, Jr.
1. He played his entire career for the Baltimore Orioles.		
2. He played his entire career for the New York Yankees.		
3. He was a first baseman.		
4. He was a shortstop and third baseman.		
5. His nickname is Iron Horse.		
6. His nickname is Iron Man.		
7. He played in 2,130 consecutive games.		
8. He played in 2,632 consecutive games.		
9. He hit 493 home runs, which is the major league record for home runs by a first baseman.		
10. He hit 324 home runs, which is the major league record for home runs by a shortstop.		
11. He retired in 2001.		
12. He retired in 1939.		
13. He won the Triple Crown in 1934.		
14. He was the league's Most Valuable Player, the All-Star Game Most Valuable Player, and a Gold Glove winner all in the same year.		

"Hoop-la"

Read each clue. Below each clue, circle the word or words that relate to the clue.

1. **first goals**

   peach baskets   water buckets   pickle barrels

2. **game creator**

   John Doe   James Naismith   Michael Jordan

3. **birthplace of the game**

   Springfield, MA   Canton, OH   Chicago, IL

4. **uniform**

   socks   high topped sneakers   gloves

5. **scoring**

   3 points   6 points   free throw

6. **ball**

   brown leather   orange plastic   red rubber

7. **playing surface**

   court   wooden   field

8. **Dream Team**

   ABA   NCAA   Olympics

9. **illegal contact**

   hook shot   foul   assist

10. **smallest team member**

    forward   guard   center

11. **one-hundred-point game**

    Wilt Chamberlain   Michael Jordan   Allen Iverson

12. **women's league**

    NBA   USWBA   WNBA

13. **professional women players**

    Sheryl Swoopes   Janet Evans   Jennifer Azzi

14. **professional NBA teams**

    Bulls   Bears   Grizzlies

15. **NBA Most Valuable Player**

    Michael Jordan   Pete Rose   Mickey Mantle

Basketball Word Chain

Use the letter clues to help you complete a chain of words related to basketball. Notice the last letter of each word becomes the first letter of the next word.

1. a ___ ___ ___ ___ t

2. t ___ ___ ___ ___ ___ ___ ___ ___ t

3. t ___ ___ ___ ___ ___ s

4. s ___ ___ t

5. t ___ ___ m

6. m ___ ___ ___ l

7. l ___ ___ ___ ___ e

8. e ___ ___ ___ w

9. w ___ ___ ___ ___ r

10. r ___ ___ ___ ___ ___ d

11. d ___ ___ k

12. k ___ y

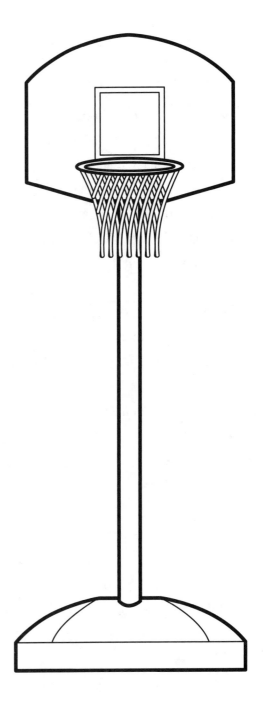

Michael Jordan

Many agree that Michael Jordan is the best basketball player that has ever lived. However, the fact is, as a sophomore, he did not even make his high school team. Yet, Michael's hard work and determination have allowed him to excel at his sport.

Part A: Michael scored 28 triple-double points during his career with the Chicago Bulls. A triple-double occurs when a player scores at least ten points, ten rebounds, and ten assists in a game. Answer the following questions and score 2 or 3 points as indicated. Can you score as many points as Michael Jordan's triple-double points?

1. How tall is Michael Jordan? _____ feet _____ inches (3 points)
2. What is Michael's wife's name? _____(3 points)
3. What is Michael's mother's name? _____(3 points)
4. What is Michael's older son's name? _____(3 points)
5. What is Michael's daughter's name? _____(3 points)
6. In what state was Michael born? _____(3 points)
7. What university did Michael attend? _____(3 points)
8. In what years did Michael play on U.S. Olympic basketball teams? _____(2 points)
9. What other professional sport did Michael try? _____(2 points)
10. What is Michael's middle name? _____(2 points)
11. What was Michael's first NBA team? _____(2 points)

Total Number of Points = _____

Part B: Calculate Michael's basketball statistics.

1. 4 x 7 – 5 = _____ (Michael's jersey number)
2. 14 + 33 + 28 – 12 = _____ (career high score in a Bulls' playoff game)
3. 78 – 30 – 20 = _____ (career triple-doubles with the Chicago Bulls)
4. (2 x 5) – 4 = _____ (Chicago Bulls championship teams)
5. (100 x 10 x 2) +1 = _____ (year Michael returned to NBA to play for Washington Wizards)
6. 997 x 2 = _____ (year Michael left the NBA to play for the Chicago White Sox AA team)
7. (6 x 9) – 13 = ___ (points Michael scored in his first Wizards' game against the New Jersey Nets)
8. (990 x 2) + 5 = _____ (year Michael was Rookie of the Year)
9. 25 + 17 + 46 – 10 = _____ (Michael's height in inches)
10. (99 x 2 x 10) +16 = _____ (year Michael starred in movie *Space Jam*)
11. (8 x 8) – 19 = _____ (jersey number Michael used after his return from baseball)
12. 104 ÷ 8 = _____ (Michael's shoe size)

Coach's Corner

Decode the meanings of these puzzles that relate to basketball.

Example: Put the p l b a l l a y = Put the ball in play.

1. t h e b a l l ↓t↓h↓e↓n↓e↓t↓ _____	2. the b a ll ↑ ↑ ↑ ↑ b o u n d s _____	3. PLAY5mins. ‾‾‾‾‾‾time‾‾‾‾ _____

4.
_____
_____
 	
s k
t   n
a   e fe ↔ et
n   e
d s
	5. l ↑ t
	   l r
	   a u
	   b o
	         c
	   e e
	   h ↑ h
	   t t
	_____
	_____
		6. t d
		   h r
		   e i
		
		   c b
		   o
		   u b
		   r l
		   t e
		_____

7.   control
  ‾‾keeptheball‾‾
 	
_____
_____
	8. h h
	   a holdthe a
	   n ball n
	   d d
	   s s
	
	_____
		9. TAKEstepsB4aP
		   ↘A S↗
		      ↘S↗

Basketball Locker Room

Use the key below to determine the value of each letter in a player's last name. Then solve the equation to determine the player's jersey number. Write the player's number on the back of the jersey. The first one has been done for you.

Key

a	e	i	o	u	b	d	l	j	r	c	h	m	n	s	t	w	y	p	k	v
1	2	3	4	5	6	7	8	9	10	11	12	13	14	15	16	17	18	19	20	21

1. **Kareem Abdul-Jabbar (Lakers)**

   $(1 + 6 + 7 + 5 + 8 + 9 + 1 + 6 + 6 + 1 + 10) - 27 =$ **33**

2. **Larry Bird (Celtics)**

   $(\underline{\quad} + \underline{\quad} + \underline{\quad} + \underline{\quad}) + 7 =$

3. **Reggie Miller (Pacers)**

   $(\underline{\quad} + \underline{\quad} + \underline{\quad} + \underline{\quad} + \underline{\quad} + \underline{\quad}) - 13 =$

4. **Vince Carter (Raptors)**

   $(\underline{\quad} + \underline{\quad} + \underline{\quad} + \underline{\quad} + \underline{\quad} + \underline{\quad}) - 35 =$

5. **Allen Iverson (76ers)**

   $(\underline{\quad} + \underline{\quad} + \underline{\quad} + \underline{\quad} + \underline{\quad} + \underline{\quad} + \underline{\quad}) \div 23 =$

6. **Karl Malone (Jazz)**

   $(\underline{\quad} + \underline{\quad} + \underline{\quad} + \underline{\quad} + \underline{\quad} + \underline{\quad}) - 10 =$

7. **Kobe Bryant (Lakers)**

   $(\underline{\quad} + \underline{\quad} + \underline{\quad} + \underline{\quad} + \underline{\quad} + \underline{\quad}) - 57 =$

8. **John Stockton (Jazz)**

   $(\underline{\quad} + \underline{\quad} + \underline{\quad} + \underline{\quad} + \underline{\quad} + \underline{\quad} + \underline{\quad} + \underline{\quad}) - 88 =$

Super Bowl Championship Teams

The first two Super Bowls were actually called the AFL-NFL (American Football League-National Football League) Championship Games. Lamar Hunt, owner of the Kansas City Chiefs, renamed the game after his children's favorite toy, the Super Ball. The Super Bowl name became official with Super Bowl III in 1969. Use the city clues to fill in the blanks with the names of teams that have won the Super Bowl. Then rearrange the circled letters to complete the last answer.

1. Kansas City __ __ __ __ __ __

2. Miami __ __ __ __ __ __ __ __

3. Chicago __ __ __ __ __

4. Washington __ __ __ __ __ __ __ __

5. St. Louis __ __ __ __

6. Pittsburgh __ __ __ __ __ __ __ __

7. Green Bay __ __ __ __ __ __ __

8. Dallas __ __ __ __ __ __ __

9. New York __ __ __ __ __ __

10. All of the players on these teams were

    __ __ __ __ __ __ __ __ __ !

Football Scoreboard Stumper

There are several ways to score in football: the touchdown (TD = 6 points), point after touchdown (PAT = 1 point), 2-point conversion (2-PT = 2 points), field goal (FG = 3 points), and safety (S = 2 points). Below are final scores for four games. Fill in the spaces with points that will add up to the final score totals. NOTE: You may use a safety only ONE time in each game.

Our Town
Final: 24 points

	1st Quarter	2nd Quarter	3rd Quarter	4th Quarter
TD				
PAT				
2-PT				
FG				
S				

Your Town
Final: 16 points

	1st Quarter	2nd Quarter	3rd Quarter	4th Quarter
TD				
PAT				
2-PT				
FG				
S				

Tigers
Final: 42 points

	1st Quarter	2nd Quarter	3rd Quarter	4th Quarter
TD				
PAT				
2-PT				
FG				
S				

Lions
Final: 30 points

	1st Quarter	2nd Quarter	3rd Quarter	4th Quarter
TD				
PAT				
2-PT				
FG				
S				

Cardinals
Final: 33 points

	1st Quarter	2nd Quarter	3rd Quarter	4th Quarter
TD				
PAT				
2-PT				
FG				
S				

Blue Jays
Final: 15 points

	1st Quarter	2nd Quarter	3rd Quarter	4th Quarter
TD				
PAT				
2-PT				
FG				
S				

Famous Former Football Players

Put the pairs of letters in order to spell the names of some professional football players. Do not rearrange the two letters in each pair. After you have named the players, name their teams. Use the city clues to help you.

1. **AI AN TR KM OY (Dallas)**

   Player: _____ Team: _____

2. **MB JI RO WN (Cleveland)**

   Player: _____ Team: _____

3. **EA MP BE RL CA LL (Houston)**

   Player: _____ Team: _____

4. **PA WA LT YT ON ER (Chicago)**

   Player: _____ Team: _____

5. **DA OU NF TS (San Diego)**

   Player: _____ Team: _____

6. **RO NN TT IE LO (San Francisco)**

   Player: _____ Team: _____

7. **JO TA EM ON NA (San Francisco)**

   Player: _____ Team: _____

8. **OZ EN ZI EW ME SO (Cleveland)**

   Player: _____ Team: _____

9. **JO HE ET SM IS AN (Washington)**

   Player: _____ Team: _____

10. **BA AN DE RR YS RS (Detroit)**

    Player: _____ Team: _____

11. **SA YE GA LE RS (Chicago)**

    Player: _____ Team: _____

12. **TA WR EN YL OR LA CE (New York)**

    Player: _____ Team: _____

13. **JO UN IT HN NY AS (Baltimore)**

    Player: _____ Team: _____

14. **ST ER NG LI SH PE AR (Green Bay)**

    Player: _____ Team: _____

15. **ST EY EV OU NG (San Francisco)**

    Player: _____ Team: _____

You Be the Official

All professional football games have seven officials. Each official has a different job. The referee, who is the final authority on the rules and gives signals on penalties, stands about 10 yards behind the quarterback.

Use the following Web site to help you name the plays and add arms to the pictures of referees to show what a referee would signal for each play: *http://www.firstbasesports.com/handsig/football/ftbhsi.htm.*

1. The ball has been run or caught across the goal line. The referee signals a . . .

_____

2. The receiver missed the ball, or it was thrown out of bounds. The referee signals an . . .

_____

3. Either team has asked to stop the clock. The referee signals a . . .

_____

4. The clock is restarted and play resumes. The referee signals . . .

_____

5. A player was hit after the whistle was blown. The referee signals a . . .

_____

6. The offensive team failed to put the ball in play before the play clock ran to zero. The referee signals a . . .

_____

7. Either team has entered the neutral zone before the start of play. The referee signals an . . .

_____

8. An offensive player has illegally held an opponent. The referee signals . . .

_____

18

What's Your Position?

A football team has eleven players on the field at one time, which sometimes include the quarterback, running back, receiver, kicker, and guard. The players must work together to score a touchdown. Read the following clues and decide which boy plays each of the five positions shown in the chart.

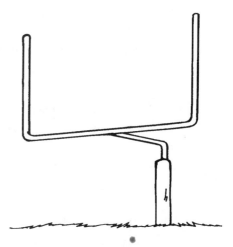

✦ Jeff lifts weights.

✦ Bobby is never late to school.

✦ Miguel has a strong leg.

✦ In the spring, Tony is an outfielder on his baseball team. He never drops the ball.

✦ Joey is a "take charge" kind of guy.

	Quarterback	Running Back	Receiver	Kicker	Guard
Jeff					
Bobby					
Miguel					
Tony					
Joey					

Newsmakers

Circle the year in which these golf events occurred.

1. Casey Martin, a handicapped golfer, sues the PGA (Professional Golfers' Association of America) for the right to ride a golf cart between shots.

   1998   **1993**   **1995**

2. Tiger Woods becomes the youngest player in history to achieve a career Grand Slam.

   1995   **2000**   **1997**

3. Jose Maria Olazabal wins his second Masters tournament.

   1997   **1993**   **1999**

4. Tiger Woods leaves college to become a professional golfer.

   1996   **1999**   **1992**

5. For the first time ever, no American won any of the four men's Grand Slam tournaments.

   1995   **1994**   **1992**

6. Corey Pavin is named PGA Player of the Year.

   1990   **1991**   **1992**

7. Ben Hogan dies at age 84.

   1998   **1997**   **1996**

8. Tom Watson resigns from the Kansas City Country Club after a Jewish applicant is denied membership.

   1987   **1989**   **1990**

9. Lee Trevino wins five senior PGA tournaments despite torn ligaments in his left thumb.

   1985   **1986**   **1992**

10. At the age of 42, Payne Stewart dies in tragic plane crash.

    1988   **1989**   **1999**

11. Greg Norman, an Australian, wins the British Open with a record 267.

    1987   **1989**   **1993**

12. Beth Daniel is named LPGA (Ladies' Professional Golf Association) Player of the Year.

    1988   **1990**   **1989**

What's Your Score?

A golfer's score is equal to the number of shots taken to get from the tee to the hole. Par is the average number of strokes a good player would need to put the ball in the cup. For this activity, par = 4.

Here are other golf scoring terms:

- ✦ *Birdie* is a score of one under par. (3 strokes)
- ✦ *Eagle* is a score of two under par. (2 strokes)
- ✦ *Ace* is the term given a hole in one. (1 stroke)
- ✦ *Bogey* is a score of one stroke above par. (5 strokes)
- ✦ *Double bogey* is a score of two above par. (6 strokes)
- ✦ *Triple bogey* is a score of three above par. (7 strokes)

Write the answer in the blank and add the numbers to determine your score.

	Correct	Incorrect	Score
1. The first game of golf was played in 1754 in _____.	par	bogey	_____
2. Two types of golf clubs are woods and _____.	birdie	double bogey	_____
3. The first shot off the tee is called a _____.	eagle	triple bogey	_____
4. High grass to the right or left of the green is called the _____.	par	bogey	_____
5. The shortest club is called a _____.	birdie	double bogey	_____
6. A _____ carries a professional golfer's bag.	eagle	triple bogey	_____
7. A regulation course has _____ holes.	par	bogey	_____
8. A player may carry _____ clubs in a golf bag.	birdie	double bogey	_____
9. Players sometimes ride between holes in _____.	eagle	triple bogey	_____

Congratulations! What is your total score? _____

Par for the Course

A regulation course has 18 holes. Each hole starts at the tee and ends at the green. There may be trees, bunkers, or hazards along the way. It is important to remember that each club has a specific purpose. To make a ball fly long and low, it is best to use a wood or low numbered iron. To make a ball rise, use high numbered clubs or irons. The term *loft* refers to how high the ball rises. A player must also consider the length of each hole when choosing appropriate clubs. Study the diagrams below and choose the best clubs to reach the green with the fewest possible shots.

Choose from these golf clubs:

1 wood (275–325 yards, 5-yard loft)   **3 iron** (150–200 yards, 20-yard loft)
3 wood (200–250 yards, 10-yard loft)   **5 iron** (100–150 yards, 40-yard loft)
5 wood (150–200 yards, 20-yard loft)   **7 iron** (70–125 yards, 60-yard loft)

Diagram A

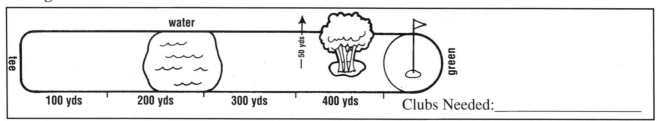

Diagram B

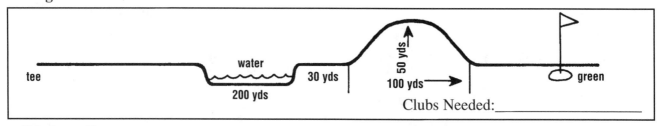

Diagram C

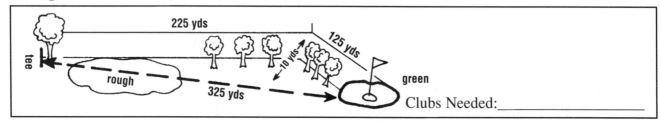

Diagram D

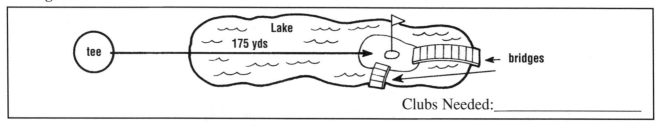

Scorecard

A golfer's score is equal to the number of shots taken to get from the tee to the hole. Par is the average number of strokes a good player would need to move the ball to the cup.

Here are some special names that golfers give certain scores.

Average = par	**1 under par = birdie**
1 above par = bogey	**2 under par = eagle**
2 above par = double bogey	**Hole-in-one = ace**
3 above par = triple bogey	

Fill in the blanks on the golfer's scorecard below. The first two have been done for you.

Look at Hole Number 1. The *par*, or average number of strokes, is 5. The golfer scored a *birdie*, which is 1 stroke under par. As a result, you know the golfer used 4 strokes to get the ball from the tee to the hole.

Now look at Hole Number 2. This golfer used 3 strokes to get the ball in the hole. The golfer scored *par*. As a result, you know that par for Hole Number 2 must have been 3 strokes.

For Hole Numbers 3, 5, 8, 10, 11, 12, 13, 16, and 18, fill in the missing numbers. For Hole Numbers 4, 7, 9, 14, 15, and 17, fill in the special names for the scores this golfer made.

Front 9	(Hole) 1	2	3	4	5	6	7	8	9
Par	5	3	4	4	5	3	4		5
Stroke	4	3		7		1	6	5	5
Type	birdie	par	bogey		eagle			bogey	

Back 9	(Hole) 10	11	12	13	14	15	16	17	18
Par	3		3	5	4	3		4	5
Stroke		6			6	1	2	3	
Type	bogey	bogey	par	birdie			eagle		par

Golfing Phenomenon: Tiger Woods

Tiger Woods might be the best golfer who has ever lived. He first took an interest in golf at 6 months of age, while watching as his father hit golf balls into a net. At age 2, Tiger demonstrated his putting skills on television during an appearance on *The Mike Douglas Show*. A year later, he shot 48 for nine holes. Tiger was featured in *Golf Digest* when he was only 5 years old.

Part A: Tiger holds the record with 52 consecutive rounds at par or better. Correctly answer these questions about Tiger Woods to score the indicated number of strokes.

1. Date of birth: _____ (4 strokes)
2. Given first name: _____ (4 strokes)
3. Parents' first names: _____ (5 strokes)
4. Mother's native country: _____ (3 strokes)
5. Height: _____ (4 strokes)
6. Birthplace: _____ (5 strokes)
7. College attended: _____ (4 strokes)
8. Date Tiger became a professional golfer: _____ (5 strokes)
9. Clothing and shoe endorsement: _____ (5 strokes)
10. Golfing equipment endorsement: _____ (4 strokes)
11. Current city and state of residence: _____ (4 strokes)
12. Non-profit organization that Tiger sponsors: _____ (5 strokes)

Total _____

Did your score match Tiger's record?

Part B: Answer the following questions about Tiger Woods's major achievements.

1. Tiger is the first golfer in history to hold all four PGA major tournament titles at the same time. What are the names of the four tournaments? _____

    _____

2. Tiger won golf's Grand Slam by winning the PGA Championship, U.S. Open, and British Open all in the year 2000. Who is the only other golfer in history to have done this in one year?

    _____

3. In 2000, Tiger won the U.S. Open by the largest margin ever. By how many strokes did he win?

    _____

4. In 1997, at age 21, Tiger became the youngest player ever to win the Masters tournament, again by the largest margin ever. By how many strokes did he win? _____

Top Gymnast

To answer the question, begin at start. Follow the arrow to move around the circle, writing every other letter. When you have completed the first two words, change your direction, begin at reverse, and write every other letter to find the last two words.

What must you have in order to be the best all around gymnast in a competition?

_____   _____   _____   _____

Gymnastics Puzzle

Complete the puzzle using the Word Bank.

Word Bank

balance beam	parallel bars	still rings
horizontal bar	Paul Hamm	uneven bars
Jaycie Phelps	pommel horse	vault
Nadia Comaneci	Shannon Miller	Vitaly Scherbo

Rebus Words

Decode the picture and letter clues to reveal gymnastics terms.

1. _____ _____

2. _____ _____   F + 👄

3. _____   P + 🚲 − B

4. _____   T + 🦆 − D

5. _____ _____   ST + ⛰ − H 💍 + S

6. _____ _____   Pom + 🐫 − CA 🐴

7. _____ _____   ⟷ B + ☆ − ST

8. _____ _____ _____

9. _____

10. _____

The Winning Vault

The vault is an event in which gymnasts perform acrobatic movements while jumping over a padded piece of equipment called a vaulting horse. Gymnasts sprint down a long runway, then jump off a springboard, which launches them into the air. They briefly places their hand on the horse, then push off and vault over it. Use this code to fill in the blanks.

G	Y	M	N	A	S	T	I	C
1	2	3	4	5	6	7	8	9

O	L	P	V	U	K	E	F
10	11	12	13	14	15	16	17

The United States women's gymnastics team was in first place at the start of the

___ ___ ___ ___ ___ ___ ___ ___ competition. All eyes were on Kerri Strug who had
13 5 14 11 7 8 4 1

___ ___ ___ ___ ___ ___ on her first landing and torn two ligaments in her
17 5 11 11 16 4

___ ___ ___ ___ ___ . She was in ___ ___ ___ ___ as she made her second
5 4 15 11 16   12 5 8 4

___ ___ ___ ___ ___ ___ ___ . Amazingly, Kerri completed the ___ ___ ___ ___ ___
5 7 7 16 3 12 7   13 5 14 11 7

and was able to ___ ___ ___ ___ ___ the landing well enough to earn a score of 9.7.
                 6 7 8 9 15

Because of her determination, the U.S. women's ___ ___ ___ ___ won the gold medal
                                                7 16 5 3

at the 1996 ___ ___ ___ ___ ___ ___ ___ ___ in ___ ___ ___ ___ ___ ___ ___ ___ , Georgia.
            10 11 2 3 12 8 9 6   5 7 11 5 4 7 5

Gymnastics Scoreboard

Part A: The perfect score for a gymnastic event is 10.00. Judges award points based on the difficulty of the element and skill with which it is accomplished. They subtract points for missed moves or flaws in a planned routine.

Nadia Comaneci, from Romania, was the first gymnast to receive a perfect score in Olympic competition. She was 14 years old when she earned seven perfect scores at the 1976 Olympic Games in Montreal. In what events did Nadia achieve perfect scores?

_____ _____ _____

Name the events in which Nadia won medals at the 1976 and 1980 Olympic Games.

Gold (1976)

_____ _____ _____

Gold (1980)

_____ _____

Silver (1976)

_____

Silver (1980)

_____ _____

Bronze (1976)

_____

Bonus: Who was the first male American gymnast to earn a perfect score (10.00) in Olympic competition? _____

Part B: Men and women compete in different gymnastics events. On a separate piece of paper, create a Venn diagram to indicate whether the following events are for men, women, or both.

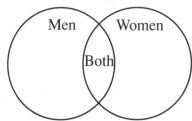

Events: pommel horse, rings, uneven bars, vault, horizontal bar, balance beam, parallel bars, floor exercise

Searching for Skaters

The Name Box below contains the first and last names of some world-famous skaters. Find the LAST names of ten of these skaters hidden in the sentences. The letters of each skater's name will appear in order. Circle the appropriate letters. Then write the name in the blank. The first one is done for you.

Name Box

Ilia Kulik	Katarina Witt	Midori Ito
Todd Eldredge	Tonya Harding	Michelle Kwan
Brian Orser	Tara Lipinski	Kurt Browning
Rudy Galindo	Scott Hamilton	Brian Boitano
Nancy Kerrigan		Dorothy Hammill

---

1. It is easy to s(lip in ski)rts that are too long. _____ *Lipinski* _____

2. She thought math was hard in grade school. _____

3. Please, sit over there. _____

4. Throw it to me. _____

5. Wave the black wand for a magical surprise. _____

6. Pass the ball to him or serve it yourself. _____

7. We usually do not mix brown in green paint. _____

8. He held red gems in his hand. _____

9. The king looked regal in double robes. _____

10. My cat Kiku likes ice cream. _____

A Great Skate

Read these clues and name the skater they describe.

Hometown: Fremont, California

Parents: Jim (dentist) and Carole (medical secretary)

Middle Name: Tsuya

Date of Birth: July 12, 1971

Achievements: Olympic gold medal, World and U.S. Champion, member of the U.S. and World Skating Hall of Fame

Career: Since 1993, has toured with Discover Card's "Stars on Ice"

What is the skater's name? _____

Add the following information about the above skater.

Siblings: _____ and _____

Partner in Pairs Competition: _____

Husband's Name: _____

After you have identified the skater, use the Date Bank to fill in the dates on this timeline, which shows her figure skating achievements. Some dates may be used more than once.

1. _____ World Junior Pairs Champion
2. _____ U.S. Pairs Champion
3. _____ Goodwill Games Champion
4. _____ World Singles Champion
5. _____ U.S. Singles Champion
6. _____ Olympic Gold Medal
7. _____ _____, _____, _____, Nickelodeon Kids' Choice for Favorite Female Athlete Awards (three years in a row)
8. _____ Inducted into the U.S. Figure Skating Hall of Fame
9. _____ Inducted into the World Figure Skating Hall of Fame

Date Bank			
1992	1991	1988	1997
1995	1989	1999	1993
2000	1994	1996	1998
			1990

Figure Skating Word Pairs

Read the clues and fill in the word pairs. Notice each word pair shares one letter.

1. circular movements

2. sliding movements

3. movements with height

4. movements off the ice

5. singles competition

6. doubles competition

7. parts of singles competition

8. parts of a skate

9. female Olympic medalists

10. two skating Brians

Bonus: These Jenkins brothers won Olympic gold medals.

Double-Checking Hockey Terms

Read the clues and identify these hockey terms. Each missing word has at least one set of double letters.

1. A player whose pass helps a teammate score has made an _____ s s _____ _____ _____.

2. A member of the opposite team is your _____ p p _____ _____ _____ _____.

3. To score, you must _____ _____ o o _____ the puck into the opposing team's goal.

4. A member of your team is your _____ _____ _____ m m _____ _____ _____.

5. If you safely move the puck to a teammate, you have made a _____ _____ s s.

6. One penalty for illegal use of a hockey stick is _____ o o _____ _____ _____ _____.

7. When a player pulls down his opponent, the penalty is called
   _____ _____ _____ p p _____ _____ _____.

8. Any play that is against the rules of hockey is called _____ l l _____ _____ _____ _____.

9. The goalie is also called a _____ _____ _____ _____ _____ e e _____ _____ _____.

10. The puck is a hard, _____ _____ b b _____ _____ disk.

11. Hockey sticks are made from _____ o o _____ .

12. A hockey team has _____ _____ _____ e e forwards on the ice at one time.

13. The person who officiates the game is the _____ _____ _____ _____ _____ e e.

14. An _____ f f _____ _____ _____ _____ _____ violation is called when a player moves ahead of the puck into the attack zone.

Bonus: An _____ n n _____ _____ _____ s s _____ _____ _____

_____ _____ _____ _____ _____ _____ _____ s s penalty is called when a player tries to

injure an opponent.

Create-a-Hockey Term

Choose one word or word part from each column (first A, then B, and finally C) to form a term related to hockey. Each word or word part will be used only once. Write the terms related to hockey in the blanks at the bottom of the page.

A	B	C
pen	ten	ling
re	al	ment
goal	fer	der
de	er	check
bod	quip	da
champ	ver	ee
mis	y	ty
e	a	men
tourn	forc	on
Can	fense	er
break	hand	ment
en	con	way
o	a	duct
pow	i	time
stick	a	play

1. _____
2. _____
3. _____
4. _____
5. _____
6. _____
7. _____
8. _____
9. _____
10. _____
11. _____
12. _____
13. _____
14. _____
15. _____

Skating Headlines

Use a reference book and the Name Bank to help you find the skater(s) involved in each of the events described in the following newspaper headlines. There are more names in the Name Bank than you will need.

1. Skating Brothers Win Olympic Gold _____

2. British Pair Dances to "Bolero" _____

3. Ukrainian Orphan Claims World Championship at 15 _____

4. Haircut Named for Skating Champ _____

5. Young Norwegian Changes Costume Tradition _____

6. Stars on Ice Head Announces Retirement _____

7. Canada Honors 2001 World Pair Champs _____

8. U.S. Girl Youngest to Win Olympic Gold _____

9. American Is European and North-American Champ _____

10. Russian Pairs Skater Dies During Practice _____

11. Skater First to Land Quad in Competition _____

12. French Woman Adds Backflip to Program _____

13. 2000 Ladies World Champion Wins Again _____

14. Young Russian Wins Men's Olympic Gold _____

15. Skater is First Asian Woman to Win World Competition _____

Name Bank

Ilia Kulik	Surya Bonaly	Todd Eldredge
Sergei Grinko	Tara Lipinski	Richard Button
Midori Ito	David Peletier	Michelle Kwan
Jamie Sale	Kurt Browning	Sonja Henie
Rudy Galindo	Oksana Baiul	Scott Hamilton
Jayne Torvill	Brian Boitano	Christopher Dean
Nancy Kerrigan	Hayes Jenkins	Dorothy Hamill
David Jenkins		

Names 'n' Numbers

Names: Use the clues to name people, places, and things related to soccer.

1. The world's greatest player of all time: _____

2. Famous stadium in Milan, Italy: _____

3. Famous Spanish player, coach, and manager: _____

4. Captain of Argentina's victorious World Cup team 1986: _____

5. England's most capped player: _____

6. Soccer's major competition around the world: _____

7. The largest stadium in the world: _____

8. Top Brazilian team: _____

Numbers: Fill in the blanks with the correct numbers.

There are _____ players on a soccer team. The most common formation being _____
        1.   2.

midfielders, _____ defenders, _____ forwards, and _____ goalkeeper.
                3.   4.   5.

A match is _____ minutes, with two _____ periods and a _____ minute half-time break.
                6.   7.   8.

The field of play is _____-_____ yards long and _____-_____ yards wide.
                9.   10.

The goal _____ feet wide and _____ feet high.
                11.   12.

The World's Best

Use the code to fill in the blanks and identify the world's best soccer player of all time.

A	C	D	E	I	M	N	O	R	S	T	B	Z	L	P	F	W
1	2	3	4	5	6	7	8	9	10	11	12	13	14	15	16	17

This soccer player was born in __ __ __ __ __ __ . At age 15, he played for the
                                      12 9 1 13 5 14

__ __ __ __ __ __ , a professional soccer club. He was a talented
10 1 7 11 8 10

__ __ __ __ __ __ __ and led his team to three __ __ __ __ __
16 8 9 17 1 9 3   17 8 9 14 3

championships. He __ __ __ __ __ __ __ in 1973, but in 1975 he
                   9 4 11 5 9 4 3

returned to play for the New York __ __ __ __ __ __
                                      2 8 10 6 8 10

The full name of the world's best soccer player is __ __ __ __ __
                                     4 3 10 8 7

__ __ __ __ __ __ __ __ __ __ __ __ __ __ __ __ __ __ ,
1 9 1 7 11 4 10 3 8 7 1 10 2 5 6 4 7 11 8

but he is best known by his nickname, __ __ __ __ .
                                15 4 14 4

Soccer Positions and Skills

Use the clues to complete the puzzle.

```
              [ ][ ][ ][D][ ][ ][ ]
                      [ ]
                      [ ]
              [ ]     [ ]
              [ ]     [ ]
[P][O][S][I][T][I][O][N][S] and [S][K][I][L][L][S]
              [ ]     [ ]        [ ]     [ ]   [ ]
                                 [ ]     [ ]   [ ]
[ ]           [ ]                [ ]     [ ]   [ ]
[ ]           [ ]                                [ ]
[ ][I][ ][ ][ ][L][ ][ ][ ]  [ ][ ][ ][ ][ ][ ][N][ ]
[ ]           [ ]                                [ ]
[ ]           [ ]     [ ]
              [ ]     [ ]
         [ ][ ][P][ ][R][ ]
              [ ]     [ ]
                      [ ]
                      [ ]
                      [ ]
```

Positions
- defender who must keep the ball out of the goal
- the last defender in front of the goalkeeper
- defender who plays farthest up field
- player who attacks with a shot at the goal
- player who must think about offense and defense equally
- another name for striker

Skills
- moving the ball with a series of short kicks
- passing the ball with the head
- moving the ball from one player to another
- stopping a dead ball with the sole of the foot
- kicking the ball for a goal

Tournament Trivia

Write an X in the appropriate column to indicate whether the event happened in the World Cup or Olympics. Then write the year in which the event occurred.

Event	World Cup	Olympics	Year
1. Bulgaria made it to the semifinals for the first time.			
2. Laszlo Kiss, from Hungary, scored a hat trick against El Salvador in just nine minutes.			
3. Diego Maradona, from Argentina, was the most fouled player in these finals.			
4. Red and yellow cards were used for the first time.			
5. Tournament finals were fully covered on television for the first time.			
6. Brazilian player Romario won both the Golden Ball and The Bronze Shoe.			
7. Mia Hamm led the United States to victory over China while playing on a sprained ankle.			
8. Diego Maradona used his hand to punch in a goal that went unnoticed by the referee.			
9. The first indoor tournament match was held in Pontiac Silverdome, which is located in Michigan.			
10. Nigeria became the first African nation to win this competition.			
11. Michelle Akers, from the United States, scored ten goals in this tournament.			
12. Spain's Under-23 team won this tournament.			

Bonus: The U.S. Women's National Team has won both of these competitions:

_____ in the year _____ and

_____ in the year _____ .

You Be the Official

Soccer games are officiated by one referee and two linesmen. The referee is responsible for issuing yellow and red cards for penalties. Linesmen assist the referee by telling when the ball is out of bounds and if the players are offside. Use the following Web site to help you name each play and add arms to the official to show the correct signal: *http://www.firstbasesports.com/handsig/soccer/scrhsi.htm*. For some signals, you may also need to draw the official's flag.

1. A player is tackled from behind. The referee signals . . .

   _____

2. A player is pushed but maintains possession of the ball. The referee signals . . .

   _____

3. Someone is called for tripping an opponent. The referee signals a . . .

   _____

4. Someone is called for unsportsmanlike conduct. The referee signals a . . .

   _____

5. A handball has occurred outside the goal box. The referee signals a . . .

   _____

6. The ball has been kicked out of bounds. The linesman signals a . . .

   _____

7. The attacking team has kicked the ball over the endline. The linesman signals a . . .

   _____

8. Either team wants to change field personnel. The linesman signals a . . .

   _____

Swimming Words

Read each word. Replace the first one or two letters to make a new word related to swimming.

1. teach — ___ ___ ___ ___ ___

2. boggles — ___ ___ ___ ___ ___ ___ ___

3. trim — ___ ___ ___ ___

4. link — ___ ___ ___ ___

5. map — ___ ___ ___

6. cave — ___ ___ ___ ___

7. hand — ___ ___ ___ ___

8. five — ___ ___ ___ ___

9. face — ___ ___ ___ ___

10. pick — ___ ___ ___ ___

11. grip — ___ ___ ___ ___

12. cater — ___ ___ ___ ___ ___

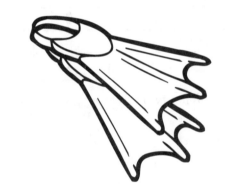

13. skipper — ___ ___ ___ ___ ___ ___ ___

14. bloat — ___ ___ ___ ___ ___

15. taps — ___ ___ ___ ___

16. chunks — ___ ___ ___ ___ ___ ___

17. tool — ___ ___ ___ ___

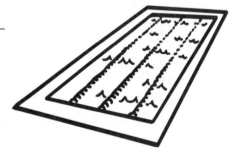

Swimming Medalists

Read these clues about men and women who have won Olympic medals in swimming. Use the Name Bank to complete the chart with the name of the swimmer that each set of clues describe.

	Number of Medals Won			Olympic Games	Swimmer's Name
	Gold	**Silver**	**Bronze**		
1.	9	1	1	1968, 1972	
2.	8	2	1	1984, 1988, 1992	
3.	4	3	1	1996, 2000	
4.	5	1	1	1984, 1988, 1992	
5.	5	1	0	1964, 1968	
6.	5	0	1	1924, 1928	
7.	8	1	1	1988, 1992, 1996, 2000	
8.	4	1	4	1984, 1988, 1992, 2000	
9.	2	6	0	1972, 1976	
10.	6	0	0	1996, 2000	
11.	3	0	3	1992, 1996	
12.	4	1	0	1988, 1992, 1996	

Bonus: What two Olympic gold medalists later went to Hollywood and starred in Tarzan movies?

_____ and _____

Name Bank

Mark Spitz
Gary Hall, Jr.
Shirley Babashoff
Matt Biondi

Tom Jager
Don Schollander
Jenny Thompson
Amy Van Dyken
Dara Torres

Johnny Weissmuller
Angel Martino
Janet Evans
Buster Crabbe

Swimming Glossary

Use the following information and the definitions provided to decode the swimming terms for this glossary. The letters of the terms have been put in alphabetical order. The first letter of each word is in bold type. When a letter is repeated, next to that letter there will be a multiplication symbol (x) and a number that indicates how many times the letter is repeated. An example has been provided for you.

Example: g i (x 2) m (x 2) n s w = swimming – what you do in water

1. **d** e i v = _____ — leap into water

2. a f l m o **p** r t = _____ — a type of diving board

3. a e **l** n s = _____ — rows in a swimming pool

4. e **g** (x 3) l o s = _____ — eye protection

5. a **c** l r w = _____ — the fastest swimming stroke

6. **b** e f l r t (x 2) u y = _____ — the hardest swimming stroke

7. a e l **r** y = _____ — race for a swim team

8. a c f (x 2) i (x 2) l **o** = _____ — judge

9. c e h i n (x 2) o r **s** y z = _____ — to match exactly

10. c k **t** u = _____ — a diving position like a cannonball

11. e i k **p** = _____ — straight legged diving position

12. a **c** m p r = _____ — a painful muscle contraction

13. e **f** l r t (x 2) u = _____ — a kick with rapid up and down leg movements

14. a h l (x 2) o s w = _____ — not the deep end of the pool

15. a **c** (x 2) h o = _____ — teacher, leader

Letter Puzzles

Analyze these groups of letters to solve the puzzles. They are in order and no letters have been omitted, but they cannot be read left to right. Patterns may be horizontal or vertical. Pay close attention to the clues provided.

1.	2.	3.
S D I W + V I G I M N N M I G water sports _____	R I V E R S L A K E S S E A S bodies of water _____	T E S T U K T H C I R G K P A I diving body positions _____
4.	5.	6.
S P I T Z E V A N S B I O N D I Olympic medalists _____	S H I S M Y R Z W I N O E I N C N D M G water ballet _____	S P R I N G B O A R D + P L A T F O R M types of diving boards _____
7.	8.	9.
B A T H I N G T I U S G O G G L E S swimmer's uniform _____	S A A P N M E D I E S N D T A needed to win _____	N V R W M L N E E S I A O E important safety rule _____

44

Take the Plunge!

A good dive must have a smooth, straight approach. The diver must lift both feet off the board at the same time and achieve enough height to assure success. Technique, timing and form must be correct in order to score points in competitive diving. Entry into the water should always be made with as little splash as possible. All dives are performed in one of these three basic positions.

- *Straight* — no bending at the waist or knees

- *Pike* — legs are straight, body is only bent at the waist

- *Tuck* — body is bent at both waist and knees, thighs are pulled up tight to the chest

Cut out the pictures from page 47 and glue them in place below and on page 46 to show the three dives in sequential order.

Straight

Take the Plunge! (cont.)

Pike

Tuck

Take the Plunge! (cont.)

Tennis Categories

Each set of clues has something in common that makes it fit into a certain category. Read the clues. Then write the name of the category next to the clues.

Clues	Category
1. love, deuce, advantage, points	
2. head, grip, strings, face	
3. tongue, sole, laces, box	
4. shoes, balls, racket, shorts	
5. serve, overhand, volley, ground	
6. Wimbledon, Davis Cup, ATP (Association of Tennis Professionals) Tour, U.S. Open	
7. clay, grass, cement, asphalt	
8. center net, service box, baseline, sidelines	
9. Andre Agassi, Pete Sampras, Michael Chang, John McEnroe	
10. Martina Navratilova, Chris Evert, Venus Williams, Steffi Graf	

Tennis Doubles

Name the players, past and present, which fit in each category.

I. Same first and last initials

A ____ ____ ____ ____   A ____ ____ ____ ____ ____

A ____ ____ ____ ____   A ____ ____ ____

B ____ ____ ____ ____   B ____ ____ ____ ____

B ____ ____ ____ ____   B ____ ____ ____

II. First name has double letters

____ ____ n n ____ ____ ____ ____ Capriati

____ ____ ____ f f ____ Graf

____ ____ d d Martin

____ ____ l l ____ ____ Jean King

III. Last name has double letters

Jan Michael ____ ____ ____ ____ ____ l l

Andy ____ ____ d d ____ ____ ____

Joseph ____ ____ ____ ____ ____ n n ____

IV. First and last names both have double letters

____ ____ b b ____   ____ ____ g g ____

____ ____ m m ____   ____ ____ n n ____ ____ ____

V. Last name has the same first and last letter

Pete S ____ ____ ____ ____ ____ s

Monica S ____ ____ ____ s

Rennae S ____ ____ ____ ____ s

Bonus: Sisters with the same last name

_____ and _____ Williams

Tennis Glossary

Read the definitions and use the clues to identify these tennis terms.

1. ☐☐☐ — a serve that cannot be returned

2. ☐☐☐☐☐☐☐☐☐ — the player who wins deuce point

3. ☐☐☐☐☐☐☐☐ — line at the end of the court, which is parallel to the net

4. ☐☐☐☐☐ — a tie at 40

5. ☐☐☐☐☐ — occurs when a ball is served into the net

6. ☐☐☐☐☐☐☐☐ — stroke played so that the palm of the hand is towards the net

7. ☐☐☐☐ ☐☐☐☐☐ — the point needed to win a game

8. ☐☐☐ — a high-arcing shot over the head of an opponent

9. ☐☐☐☐ — zero or nothing

10. ☐☐☐☐☐ — the best of a three-set or five-set format

11. ☐☐☐ — runs through the middle of the court and is 3 feet high and made of nylon

12. ☐☐☐☐☐ — name given to a long exchange of strokes

13. ☐☐☐☐☐ — stroke used to start each point

14. ☐☐☐ — usually first to win six games, except in the case of a tie, when a tie-breaker is played

15. ☐☐☐☐☐☐ — when a player hits the ball before it bounces

Word Bank

ace	foot fault	overhead
advantage	forehand	rally
baseline	game point	serve
court	lob	set
deuce	love	slice
fault	match	volley
	net	

50

10 "S" Stars

Part A: Fill in the first or last names of these tennis stars past and present. Notice that all of the missing names begin with the letter S. Then indicate the country each player represents.

Name	Country
1. Pete S ___ ___ ___ ___ ___ ___	
2. S ___ ___ ___ ___ ___ Williams	
3. Monica S ___ ___ ___ ___	
4. S ___ ___ ___ ___ ___ Graf	
5. S ___ ___ ___ ___ ___ Edberg	
6. S ___ ___ ___ ___ ___ ___ ___ Lareau	
7. Gabriela S ___ ___ ___ ___ ___ ___ ___	
8. Rennae S ___ ___ ___ ___ ___	
9. S ___ ___ ___ Smith	
10. Manuel S ___ ___ ___ ___ ___ ___	

Part B: The Grand Slam of tennis consists of four international, open tournaments. Write the tournaments next to the months in which they occur.

1. January: _____

2. May/June: _____

3. June/July: _____

4. August/September: _____

Part C: Answer the following questions.

1. Which woman won the Grand Slam in 1988? _____

2. Which man won the Grand Slam in both 1962 and 1969? _____

3. Which woman has won nine Wimbledon singles titles? _____

4. Which man has won seven Wimbledon singles titles? _____

Tennis "Term-inator"

Part A: Change one vowel in each word to create a tennis term.

1. nut → _____

2. live → _____

3. bell → _____

4. black → _____

5. ice → _____

6. shut → _____

7. valley → _____

8. lit bull → _____

9. strike → _____

Part B: Change the initial consonant in each word to create a tennis term.

1. job → _____

2. roach → _____

3. packet → _____

4. hatch → _____

5. nerve → _____

6. drip → _____

7. jingles → _____

8. candle → _____

9. wet → _____

What a Racket!

All tennis rackets were made of wood before the 1960s. These rackets had a small hitting area and weighed about 14 ounces. Aluminum rackets came into accepted use in the late 1960s. They were lighter than wood, giving the player a faster swing but less control. In 1976, the Prince racket was introduced. It had a much larger hitting surface so players did not have to hit the ball perfectly to be successful. Today, most rackets are made of fiberglass and graphite.

Part A: The parts of the tennis racket shown below are improperly labeled. Correct them.

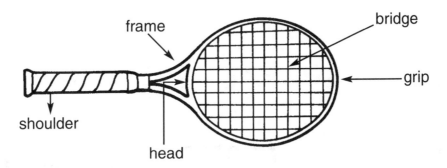

Part B: Different kinds of rackets are used for other sports. Label each of the following rackets to indicate whether they are used for badminton, racquetball, table tennis, or squash.

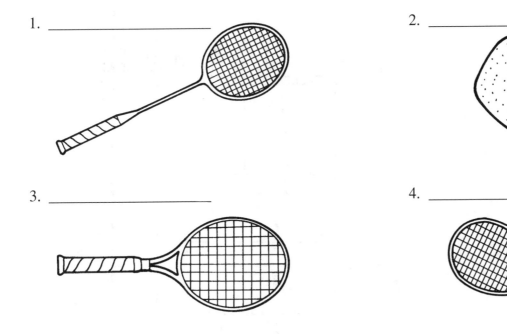

1. _____

2. _____

3. _____

4. _____

"Virtual" Point

Label these parts on the diagram of a tennis court shown below.

✦ net   ✦ singles sideline   ✦ service line

✦ baseline

Joe and Shawn are playing tennis. Use the grid on the tennis court diagram to plan their plays.

Joe begins with a serve to B-3.

Shawn returns to _____ .

Joe returns to _____ .

Shawn returns to _____ .

Joe returns to _____ .

Shawn returns to _____ .

Score Point goes to _____ .

Word Within Words

Use the definitions in parentheses as clues to help you complete each term that is related to track-and-field sports. The missing letters in each term spell a word.

1. ath _____ _____ _____ ics (Olympic name for track and field category)

2. s _____ _____ _____ put (heavy metal ball)

3. l _____ _____ g (jumping event)

4. de _____ _____ _____ hlon (ten event sport)

5. d _____ _____ c _____ _____ (round, flat object)

6. e _____ _____ _____ _____ s (individual sports)

7. t _____ _____ _____ le (jumping event)

8. h _____ _____ st _____ _____ _____ _____ (leg muscle)

9. wal _____ _____ _____ _____ (not running)

10. s _____ _____ _____ _____ _____ er (short-distance runner)

11. g _____ _____ _____ (equipment)

12. cl _____ _____ _____ s (track shoes)

13. ma _____ _____ _____ h _____ _____ (longest race)

14. dr _____ _____ _____ s (practice exercises)

15. ba _____ _____ _____ (relay stick)

You've Got Mail

Name a track and field athlete who might use each of these e-mail addresses.

1. 26mi@go-run.com

    _____

2. Olygold@lng-jmp.com

    _____

3. hi-speed@champ1.com

    _____

4. discusguy@u-toss-em.com

    _____

5. winner@jumpx3.com

    _____

6. no1@p_vault.com

    _____

7. tops@H_jump.com

    _____

8. star@track/field.com

    _____

9. speedyguy@sprntcty.com

    _____

10. trkstr@fastr.com

    _____

11. sht.put@big-toss.com

    _____

12. racergirl@speedy.com

    _____

13. bigman@decath.com

    _____

14. bestgal@hurdlejmpr.com

    _____

15. c-ctyguy@run-on.com

    _____

56

How Do You Measure Up?

Part A: Determine the measurement for each item. Round each answer to the nearest meter or foot.
Use 1 meter = 3.3 feet = 39 inches.

1. The first sprint in the 776 B.C. Olympics was 192 meters long.

    | 192 meters = _____ feet |

2. "World's Fastest Human" is the title given the winner of the 100-meter sprint.

    | 100 meters = _____ feet |

3. Men athletes run 110-meter hurdles.

    | 110 meters = _____ feet |

4. A popular indoor race is 60 meters long.

    | 60 meters = _____ feet |

5. The 1500-meter race is known as the metric mile. However, the measurement is not exactly a
    mile. Find the difference between a standard mile and a metric mile.

    | 1500 meters = _____ feet |
    | 1 mile = _____ feet |
    | The difference between a metric mile and a standard mile is _____ feet. |

Part B: Read the information about these track-and-field record holders. Convert the measurements
from meters to feet to the nearest hundredth. Use 1 meter = 3.3 feet = 39 inches.

1. Al Oerter, from the United States, was the first man to throw the discus more than 200 feet.

    | 200 feet = _____ meters |

2. Sergei Bubka, from the Ukraine, was the first pole vaulter to clear 20 feet.

    | 20 feet = _____ meters |

3. Michael Johnson, from the United States, set the world record (19.32 seconds) at the 1996 Atlanta
    Games for the 200-meter sprint.

    | 200 meters = _____ feet |

4. Randy Barnes, from the United States, holds the standing outdoor shot put record with a throw of
    75 feet, 10 inches.

    | 75 feet, 10 inches = _____ meters |

5. Carl Lewis, from the United States, won his ninth Olympic gold medal with a long jump of 27
    feet, 11 inches.

    | 27 feet, 11 inches = _____ meters |

6. Olympian Kate Schmidt, from the United States, holds the record for a javelin throw of 227 feet,
    5 inches.

    | 227 feet, 5 inches = _____ meters |

7. Bob Beamon, from the United States, holds the Olympic record for a long jump of 29 feet, 2.5
    inches.

    | 29 feet, 2.5 inches = _____ meters |

Track-and-Field Events

Use the answers in the circles to fill in the blanks. Cross off each answer as you use it. The answer that is left in the circles will complete the bonus sentence.

1. A short race

2. 800–5000 meter races

3. Name of 192-meter sprint included in first Olympic Games

4. Race for a four member team

5. Leap over a bar

6. L-shaped fences that runners jump over

7. Race that includes hurdles and water jumps

8. 26.2-mile run

9. Hop, step, and jump

10. Aided high jump

11. Sport in which athlete heaves a metal ball as far as possible

12. A flat circle made of metal and wood

13. A spear thrown for distance

14. Two day multi-event competition for women

15. Two day multi-event competition for men

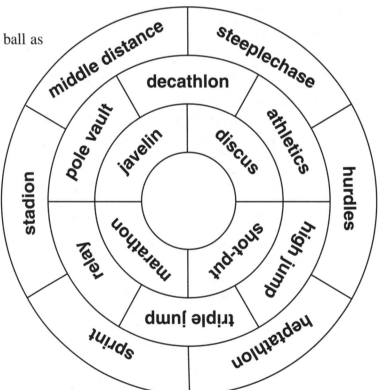

Bonus: Another name for track-and-field events is _____.

Volleyball Rules

Change the boldfaced words to correct the information in this paragraph about volleyball rules.

James Morgan, a YMCA instructor, created the game
    (1)
of volleyball in 1895. It was first included as an

official team sport in the 1964 Olympic Games.

Volleyball is played on a **field**, separated into two
                          (2)
halves by a **rope**. There are two opposing teams, one
            (3)
on each side of the court. There are

nine players on each team. They stand in **three** rows
  (4)   (5)
with three players in each row. In volleyball,

players play all **five** positions, rotating
                  (6)
counterclockwise each time their side gets the serve.
    (7)
The server may hit the **net** overhand or underhand but
                        (8)
must use one hand when striking. The receiving team

may use as many as **four** hits to return the ball. The
                    (9)
ball may be hit with the **feet** and fists. It is possible
                          (10)
to **score a point** for reaching over the net to play ball.
   (11)
A team receives a **time out** if they score on the
                  (12)
opposing team's a serve. There are three or five

games in a **rally**, depending on the skill level of the
           (13)
players.

Only the serving team can score a point. The winner

is the first team to score **20** points, with at least a
                           (14)
three-point advantage.
  (15)

1. _____

2. _____

3. _____

4. _____

5. _____

6. _____

7. _____

8. _____

9. _____

10. _____

11. _____

12. _____

13. _____

14. _____

15. _____

Oops, It's All My Fault!

Every sport has rules. Volleyball officials make sure the game is played fairly. Penalties are called faults. Below there is a list of errors that may occur in sporting events. Circle the item number of each error that results in a fault in volleyball.

1. You allow the ball to touch the floor.

2. You touch the ball more than twice in a row.

3. Your team hits the ball more than three times in a row.

4. You hit an opponent with your stick.

5. You change lanes while running.

6. You charge at an opponent and strike him with your helmet.

7. You grab an opponent's facemask.

8. You trip while shooting a basket.

9. You make an improper serve.

10. You hold, then throw the ball.

11. You trip an opponent as he attempts to shoot a basket.

12. You hit a fly ball that is caught by an infielder.

Bonus

Add together the item numbers that you circled above to find how many points are necessary for a team to win a non-deciding game with a minimum two-point advantage and no scoring cap in the rally scoring system. _____

Now subtract ten from the above sum to find the number of points needed to win a deciding game with a minimum two-point advantage and no scoring cap in the rally scoring system. _____

Volleyball Glossary

Use the following information and the definitions provided to decode the volleyball terms for this glossary. The letters of the terms have been put in alphabetical order. The first letter of each word is in bold type. When a letter is repeated, next to that letter there will be a multiplication symbol (x) and a number that indicates how many times the letter is repeated. An example has been provided for you.

Example: a b e l (x 4) o **v** y = volleyball — the name of a game with a net that splits the court into two halves

1. a c h **m** t = _____ — a predetermined number of games

2. a l (x 2) **r** y = _____ — the time when the ball is in play

3. i **k** l (x 2) = _____ — a shot that can't be returned

4. **c** o r t u = _____ — the area where the game is played

5. e i k p **s** = _____ — a rapid hit that sends the ball hard down onto the court

6. **a** (x 2) c e k r t (x 2) = _____ — a player in the front court

7. a **f** l t u = _____ — an illegal move or play

8. a c i o n t **s** = _____ — a punishment given by the referee for illegal behavior

9. e (x 4) f **r** (x 2) = _____ — an official

10. b e i **s** (x 2) t (x 3) u (x 2) = _____ — an extra player who waits on the bench

11. a **b** c e h = _____ — a place to play in sand

12. a d e (x 2) **k** n s p = _____ — protective knee coverings

13. a i o (x 2) n **r** t (x 2) = _____ — clockwise movement of the serving team

14. a e (x 2) h **l** r t = _____ — ball covering

15. e (x 2) i o **m** n (x 2) t (x 3) = _____ — the original name for volleyball

Team Sports Stars Anagrams

Anagrams are words or phrases formed by rearranging the letters in another word. Rearrange the words to spell the names of popular athletes. Use the initials and playing positions to help you.

Baseball

1. alarm robe root → R _____ A _____ (second baseman)

2. lark rib yarn → B _____ L _____ (shortstop)

3. tee red jerk → D _____ J _____ (shortstop)

4. moss am say → S _____ S _____ (outfielder)

5. clerk pin jar → C _____ R _____ (shortstop, third baseman)

Basketball

1. cake trip wing → P _____ E _____ (center)

2. car rice vent → V _____ C _____ (forward)

3. an equal ill hose → S _____ O _____ (center)

4. cent it pops pie → S _____ P _____ (forward)

5. all one mark → K _____ M _____ (forward)

Football

1. join sunny hat → J _____ U _____ (quarterback)

2. hen law joy → J _____ E _____ (quarterback)

3. main do ran → D _____ M _____ (quarterback)

4. sad iron seen → D _____ S _____ (cornerback)

5. all dirt serve → T _____ D _____ (running back)

Team-Sports Analogies

To complete an analogy, you must first determine the relationship between the given items. The relationship may be sport to equipment, sport to location, etc.

Example: hockey : net :: basketball : hoop

This analogy is read as "hockey is to net as basketball is to hoop."

1. _____ : United States :: rugby : England

2. baseball : _____ :: ice hockey : goalie

3. soccer : _____ :: baseball : umpire

4. baseball : cap :: football : _____

5. _____ : club :: baseball : bat

6. baseball : ball :: hockey : _____

7. ice hockey : _____ :: baseball : spikes

8. baseball : manager :: football : _____

9. basketball team : five :: ice hockey team : _____

10. volleyball : _____ :: soccer : foot

11. football : game :: _____ : match

12. _____ : Super Bowl :: baseball : World Series

Bonus

1. _____ : James Naismith :: _____ : Abner Doubleday :: volleyball : William Morgan

2. basketball: _____ :: baseball : diamond :: football: _____

3. football :_____ :: _____ : Tigers :: _____ : Pistons :: hockey : Red Wings

---

Individual-Sports Analogies

To complete an analogy, you must first determine the relationship between the given items. The relationship may be sport to equipment, sport to location, etc.

Example: suit : swimming :: leotard : gymnastics

This analogy is read as "suit is to swimming as leotard is to gymnastics."

1. barbells : lifting :: discus : _____

2. board : _____ :: trampoline : tumbling

3. freestyle : swimming :: sprint : _____

4. salchow : figure skating :: slalom : _____

5. _____ : cross-country skiing :: height : pole vaulting

6. _____ : golf :: racket : tennis

7. course : golf :: _____ : tennis

8. target : _____ :: pocket : billiards

9. _____ : skating score :: 10 : gymnastics score

10. horse : ride :: rifle : _____

11. lift : weight :: _____ : bicycle

12. elbow : pads :: _____ : helmet

Bonus:

1. strike/spare : bowling :: bogey/birdie : _____ : love/deuce : _____

2. archery : arrow :: bowling : _____ :: discus : _____

3. Greco-Roman, freestyle, Sumo : _____ :: alpine, freestyle, cross country : _____

Awesome American Athletes
from the Past

Circle the words in Columns 2 and 3 that describe the record-setting athletes listed in Column 1.

Column 1	Column 2	Column 3
1. Wilt Chamberlain	100 points 89 points 14 fouls	March 2, 1962 September 3, 1970 February 17, 1968
2. Nolan Ryan	catcher pitcher first baseman	15 seasons 18 seasons 27 seasons
3. Dick Button	boxer figure skater soccer	first American Olympic gold medal three heavyweight titles winning goalie
4. Tony Dorsett	quarterback running back cornerback	most touchdown passes 99-yard touchdown most sacks in a single season
5. Jack Nicklaus	runner golfer tennis player	record hurdler oldest to win Masters title youngest to win Wimbledon
6. Mary Lou Retton	goalie sprinter gymnast	most points in a game all-around Olympic gold medal fastest time in 200 meters
7. Wayne Gretzsky	center quarterback guard	all-time leading NHL scorer all-time leading NBA rebounds all-time leading NFL touchdowns
8. Mark Spitz	swimmer diver slider	9 Olympic gold medals 3 Olympic silver medals 7 Olympic gold medals
9. Arthur Ashe	1975 1968 1970	World Cup Wimbledon Super Bowl
10. Muhammed Ali	boxer pitcher running back	Athlete of the Century Rookie of the Year Most Valuable Player

Sort the Pros

Write the name of each professional sports team under the appropriate heading of the chart.

National Hockey League (NHL)
_____
_____
_____
_____

National Football League (NFL)
_____
_____
_____
_____

National Basketball Association (NBA)
_____
_____
_____
_____

Major League Baseball (MLB)
_____
_____
_____
_____

Team Box

- New York Rangers
- Cincinnati Reds
- Los Angeles Lakers
- Buffalo Bills
- San Francisco 49ers
- Detroit Red Wings
- Seattle Mariners
- Boston Celtics
- Chicago Bulls
- Dallas Cowboys
- Boston Bruins
- New York Yankees

Identifying Unusual Sports

Use the Word Bank to help identify these unusual sports.

Word Bank		
cycling	cricket	lacrosse
broomball	fencing	polo
croquet	karate	rugby
squash	luge	table tennis

1. It is played on an ice rink and requires safety gear. Players use a broom to slide a ball into the opposing team's goal. The sport is _____ .

2. This sport is popular in England. Teams use a flat bat to strike a ball made of hard cork. Announcers describe the action with terms like "googly" and "donkey drop." The sport is

    _____ .

3. Players use mallets to hit wooden balls through wickets in this lawn game. The sport is

    _____ .

4. Team members ride in drafts in this sport requiring speed and endurance. The lightweight metal equipment may have 18–21 gears. The sport is _____ .

5. The foil, epee, and sabre are three instruments used in this sport that began in medieval times. The sport is _____ .

6. Training in a "dojo" and wearing a "gi," participants in this sport earn different color belts to show their skill level. The sport is _____ .

7. Players use a crosse to get a solid rubber ball into the opposing team's goal. The sport is

    _____ .

8. Spiked gloves help the sliders grip the icy surface in this form of sled racing. The sport is

    _____ .

9. Players on horseback use mallets to strike a ball into the opponents' net during games, which are six chukkers in length. The sport is _____ .

10. A heavy, oval ball is advanced down the pitch into the opposition's try zone in this game. Teams are divided into groups called the "pack" and the "wing." The sport is _____ .

11. Two or four players use rackets and the walls of their court to play caroms. They must keep their shots above the tin. The sport is _____ .

12. This indoor sport requires small wooden paddles and a celluloid ball. A net is stretched across the center of a table. The sport is _____ .

Name the Pro Teams

> NFL = National Football League
>
> MLB = Major League Baseball
>
> NBA = National Basketball Association
>
> NHL = National Hockey League

Part A: Write the professional sports team whose name has the opposite meaning of the words in the list.

1. Dwarfs _____ (NFL)
2. Peacemakers _____ (NBA)
3. Sinners _____ (NFL)
4. Cowgirls _____ (NFL)
5. Confederates _____ (MLB)
6. Queens _____ (NBA)
7. Moons _____ (NBA)
8. Coolness _____ (NBA)
9. Bears _____ (NBA)
10. Tame _____ (NHL)

Part B: Write the professional sports team whose name rhymes with the words in the list.

1. Dangers _____ (MLB)
2. Skins _____ (MLB)
3. Tubs _____ (MLB)
4. Volts _____ (NFL)
5. Sets _____ (NFL)
6. Hams _____ (NFL)
7. Towns _____ (NFL)
8. Pockets _____ (NBA)
9. Slippers _____ (NBA)
10. Cornets _____ (NBA)

Sports Categories

Cross out one term in each list that does not fit with the others. Then name the sport that the remaining terms describe.

1. pitcher, catcher, quarterback, World Series _____

2. key, court, home run, rebound _____

3. hook, jab, ring, singlet _____

4. axel, salchow, lutz, Frisbee™ _____

5. field goal, end zone, toe pick, linemen _____

6. woods, irons, putter, racket _____

7. umpire, pommel horse, balance beam, vault _____

8. rink, skates, ball, goalie _____

9. Nordic, Alpine, slalom, puck _____

10. World Cup, striker, service line, offside _____

11. freestyle, pike, butterfly, backstroke _____

12. fault, lob, topspin, squash _____

13. stroke, hurdle, sprint, relay _____

14. squat, dive, clean and jerk, snatch _____

15. bull's eye, crossbow, club, arrow _____

Categorically Speaking

Each category is described by a list of terms. One term does not belong. Cross out the term in each list that does not fit with the others.

1. **Places to play** — field, green, court, television

2. **Ways to score** — touchdown, basket, home run, clock

3. **Things to hit** — car, puck, shuttlecock, target

4. **Things to throw** — ball, horseshoe, basket, javelin

5. **Things to swing** — club, sticks, football, racket

6. **Things to wear** — shoulder pads, helmet, announcer, jersey

7. **Parts of a boat** — keel, neck, spinnacker, hull

8. **Parts of a racket** — foot, neck, face, head

9. **Athletics competition** — running, jumping, skipping, throwing

10. **Cycling competition** — sprint, time trials, road races, hurdles

11. **Equestrian competition** — dressage, steeplechase, cycling, show jumping

12. **Ball games** — archery, soccer, squash, bowling

13. **Winter sports** — skiing, curling, luge, marathon

14. **Water sports** — swimming, rowing, skating, surfing

15. **Decision-makers** — spectator, judge, official, umpire

Early Names of Common Games

Write the modern name for each of these early games. Use the clues to help you find the answers.

1. **Bandy Ball** → H ___ ___ ___ ___ ___

2. **Ping Pong** → T ___ ___ ___ ___   T ___ ___ ___ ___ ___

3. **Sphairistike** → T ___ ___ ___ ___ ___

4. **Paganica** → G ___ ___ ___

5. **Baggataway** → L ___ ___ ___ ___ ___ ___ ___

6. **Pok-ta-pok** → B ___ ___ ___ ___ ___ ___ ___ ___

7. **Paddle-raquets** → R ___ ___ ___ ___ ___ ___ ___ ___ ___

8. **Pall Mall** → C ___ ___ ___ ___ ___ ___

9. **Stoolball** → C ___ ___ ___ ___ ___ ___

10. **Rounders** → B ___ ___ ___ ___ ___ ___ ___

11. **Shrove-groat** → S ___ ___ ___ ___ ___ ___ ___ ___ ___ ___

12. **Poona** → B ___ ___ ___ ___ ___ ___ ___

13. **Paume** → H ___ ___ ___ ___ ___ ___ ___

14. **Episkyros** → S ___ ___ ___ ___ ___

15. **Mintonette** → V ___ ___ ___ ___ ___ ___ ___ ___ ___

Plates of the Pros

Some car license plates give clues about their owners. Decode the clues on these imaginary license plates.

Bonus: Name a professional athlete to whom each imaginary license plate could belong.

NHL CAPT	NBA CNTR	GR8 SK8
1. _____ _____	2. _____ _____	3. _____ _____

HOT SHOT	TALL GUY	GR8 SHOT
4. _____ _____	5. _____ _____	6. _____ _____

3PT SHOT	NFL BACK	MLB FLDR
7. _____ _____	8. _____ _____	9. _____ _____

Q BACK	H R KING	1 2 3 OUT
10. _____ _____	11. _____ _____	12. _____ _____

72

Points of Origin

Write the name of the country where each sport began. Use a reference book and the Word Bank to help with the answers.

Sport	Country of Origin
1. Tennis	
2. Badminton	
3. Ice Hockey	
4. Basketball	
5. Baseball	
6. Golf	
7. Ice Skating	
8. Bobsled	
9. Martial Arts	
10. Athletics	
11. Cycling	
12. Fencing	
13. Boxing	
14. Jai-Alai	
15. Cricket	

Word Bank

France	Canada	Scotland
Norway	Japan	Spain
England	United States	Greece
	Switzerland	

Winning Women

Name the sport in which each of these winning women athletes participated. Write an O next to each Olympian. Three women in the list are not Olympians.

Athlete	Sport	Olympians
1. Althea Gibson		
2. Sonja Henie		
3. Brandi Chastain		
4. Nancy Lopez		
5. Billie Jean King		
6. Esther Williams		
7. Wilma Rudolph		
8. Mary Lou Retton		
9. Jackie Joyner-Kersee		
10. Mia Hamm		
11. Joan Benoit		
12. Flo Hyman		
13. Janet Evans		
14. Bonnie Blair		
15. Picabo Street		

Bonus: Use the item numbers of the three women who are not Olympians to solve the following equation and to determine the total number of goals scored by the 1996 U.S. Olympic women's soccer team in their gold medal winning game against China.

_____ + _____ – _____ = ☐

Answer Key

Baseball
Nicknames Past and Present (page 3)
1. Ty Cobb
2. Joe DiMaggio
3. Lou Gehrig
4. Reggie Jackson
5. Willie Mays
6. Pete Rose
7. Babe Ruth
8. Henry Aaron
9. Roger Clemens
10. Joe Jackson
11. Jim Hunter
12. Ernie Banks
13. Frank Thomas
14. Ken Griffey, Jr.
15. Cal Ripken, Jr.

Baseball Equations (page 4)
1. Players on a Baseball Team
2. Feet between Bases
3. Strikes that make an Out
4. Hits in a No-Hitter
5. Innings in a Game
6. Runs for a Grand Slam
7. Base Paths on a Diamond
8. Games in the World Series
9. Teams in the American League
10. Teams in the National League
11. Sides on Home Plate
12. Balls that make a Walk
13. Weight of Baseball
14. Umpires per Game
15. Managers per Team

Links to Baseball Terminology (page 5)
Accept all reasonable answers.
Suggested answers:
1. manor
2. rut, hut
3. bin, bit
4. tear
5. clay, clam
6. patch
7. hose, host
8. foal, coal, coat, boat
9. pair, pain
10. sane, lane, lone
11. came, case
12. bay, say, sly

Baseball Brothers (page 6)
1. Aaron
2. Alou
3. Boone
4. Canseco
5. Giambi
6. Guerrero
7. Gwynn
8. Larkin
9. Martinez
10. Niekro
11. Ripken
12. Sherry

Calling All Fans (page 7)
1. Orioles
2. Yankees
3. Indians
4. Tigers
5. Royals
6. Angels
7. Mariners
8. Rangers
9. Braves
10. Marlins
11. Cubs
12. Pirates
13. Cardinals
14. Padres
15. Giants

Baseball's Triple Crown (page 8)
1956 — Mantle
1934 — Gehrig
1933 — Klein
1942 + 1947 — Williams
1912 — Zimmerman
1909 — Cobb
1922 + 1925 — Hornsby
1966 — Robinson
1937 — Medwick
Bonus: Carl Yastrzemski

The "Streak" (page 9)
1, 4, 6, 8, 10, 11, 14: Ripken, Jr.
2, 3, 5, 7, 9, 12, 13: Gehrig

Basketball
"Hoop-la" (page 10)
1. peach baskets
2. James Naismith
3. Springfield, MA
4. socks, high topped sneakers
5. 3 points, free throw
6. brown leather
7. court, wooden
8. Olympics
9. foul
10. guard
11. Wilt Chamberlain
12. WNBA
13. Sheryl Swoopes, Jennifer Azzi
14. Bulls, Grizzlies
15. Michael Jordan

Basketball Word Chain (page 11)
1. assist
2. tournament
3. tickets
4. shot
5. team
6. medal
7. league
8. elbow
9. winner
10. rebound
11. dunk
12. key

Michael Jordan (page 12)
Part A
1. 6 feet 6 inches
2. Juanita
3. Deloris
4. Jeffrey
5. Jasmine
6. New York
7. University of North Carolina
8. 1984 and 1992
9. baseball
10. Jeffrey
11. Chicago Bulls

Part B
1. 23
2. 63
3. 28
4. 6
5. 2001
6. 1994
7. 41
8. 1985
9. 78
10. 1996
11. 45
12. 13

Coach's Corner (page 13)
1. The ball passes through the net.
2. Throw the ball out of bounds.
3. Play five minutes overtime
4. Stand with knees bent and feet apart.
5. Move the ball up the court.
6. Dribble down the court.
7. Keep the ball under control.
8. Hold the ball between two hands.
9. Take short steps before a bounce pass.

Basketball Locker Room (page 14)
1. 33
2. 33
3. 31
4. 15
5. 3
6. 32
7. 8
8. 12

Answer Key

Football

Super Bowl Championship Teams (page 15)

1. Chiefs
2. Dolphins
3. Bears
4. Redskins
5. Rams
6. Steelers
7. Packers
8. Cowboys
9. Giants
10. champions

Football Scoreboard Stumper (page 16)
Answers will vary.

Famous Former Football Players (page 17)

1. Troy Aikman, Cowboys
2. Jim Brown, Browns
3. Earl Campbell, Oilers
4. Walter Payton, Bears
5. Dan Fouts, Chargers
6. Ronnie Lott, 49ers
7. Joe Montana, 49ers
8. Ozzie Newsome, Browns
9. Joe Theissman, Redskins
10. Barry Sanders, Lions
11. Gale Sayers, Bears
12. Lawrence Taylor, Giants
13. Johnny Unitas, Colts
14. Sterling Sharpe, Packers
15. Steve Young, 49ers

You Be the Official (page 18)

1. touchdown
2. incomplete pass
3. time out
4. time in
5. personal foul
6. delay of game
7. offside
8. holding

What's Your Position? (page 19)
Jeff — guard
Bobby — running back
Miguel — kicker
Tony — receiver
Joey — quarterback

Golf

Newsmakers (page 20)

1. 1998
2. 2000
3. 1999
4. 1996
5. 1994
6. 1991
7. 1997
8. 1990
9. 1992
10. 1999
11. 1993
12. 1990

What's Your Score? (page 21)

1. Scotland
2. irons
3. drive
4. rough
5. putter
6. caddie
7. 18
8. 14
9. cart

Par for the Course (page 22)
Diagram A — Clubs Needed: 1 wood, 7 iron
Diagram B — Clubs Needed: 3 wood, 7 iron
Diagram C — Clubs Needed: 3 wood, 5 iron
Diagram D — Clubs Needed: 5 wood OR 3 iron

Score Card (page 23)
Front 9
Hole Number 3: Stroke = 5
Hole Number 4: Type = triple bogey
Hole Number 5: Stroke = 3
Hole Number 6: Type = ace
Hole Number 7: Type = double bogey
Hole Number 8: Par = 4
Hole Number 9: Type = par
Back 9
Hole Number 10: Stroke = 4
Hole Number 11: Par = 5
Hole Number 12: Stroke = 3
Hole Number 13: Stroke = 4
Hole Number 14: Type = double bogey
Hole Number 15: Type = ace
Hole Number 16: Par = 4
Hole Number 17: Type = birdie
Hole Number 18: Stroke = 5

Golfing Phenomenon: Tiger Woods (page 24)
Part A:

1. 12/30/75
2. Eldrick
3. Earl and Kultida
4. Thailand
5. 6 feet 1 inch
6. Cypress, California
7. Stanford University
8. 8/28/96
9. Nike
10. Titleist
11. Orlando, Florida
12. Tiger Woods Foundation

Part B:

1. The Masters
2. Ben Hogan, 1953
3. 15 strokes
4. 12 strokes.

Gymnastics

Top Gymnast (page 25)
the highest total score

Gymnastics Puzzle (page 26)

1. Vitaly Scherbo
2. Paul Hamm
3. Shannon Miller
4. Jaycie Phelps
5. Nadia Comaneci
6. parallel bars
7. pommel horse
8. balance beam
9. vault
10. horizontal bar
11. uneven bars
12. still rings

Rebus Words (page 27)

1. leg swing
2. back flips
3. pike
4. tuck
5. still rings
6. pommel horse
7. horizontal bar
8. six man team
9. cartwheel
10. handspring

The Winning Vault (page 28)
vaulting
fallen
ankle
pain
attempt
vault
stick
team
Olympics
Atlanta

Gymnastics Scoreboard (page 29)
Part A:
Perfect Scores: uneven bars, balance beam, floor exercises
Olympic Medals
Gold (1976) — uneven bars, balance beam, all-around
Gold (1980) — balance beam, floor exercises
Silver (1976) — team
Silver (1980) — all around, team
Bronze (1976) — floor exercises
Bonus: Mitch Gaylord
Part B:
Men: pommel horse, rings, parallel bars, horizontal bar
Both: vault, floor exercise
Women: balance beam, uneven bars

Skating and Hockey

Searching for Skaters (page 30)
1. Lipinski
2. Harding
3. Ito
4. Witt
5. Kwan
6. Orser
7. Browning
8. Eldredge
9. Galindo
10. Kulik

A Great Skate (page 31)
Skater: Kristi Yamaguchi
Siblings: Lori and Brett
Partner: Rudy Galindo
Husband: Bret Hedican
1. 1988
2. 1989
3. 1990
4. 1991
5. 1992
6. 1992
7. 1996, 1997, 1998
8. 1998
9. 1999

Figure Skating Word Pairs (page 32)
1. spin, turn
2. glide, skate
3. jump, leap
4. lift, throw
5. women, men
6. pairs, ice dancing
7. technical, free skate
8. boot, blade
9. Kwan, Lipinski
10. Orser, Boitano
Bonus: Hayes, David

Double-Checking Hockey Terms (page 33)
1. assist
2. opponent
3. shoot
4. teammate
5. pass
6. hooking
7. tripping
8. illegal
9. goalkeeper
10. rubber
11. wood
12. three
13. referee
14. offsides
Bonus: unnecessary roughness

Create-a-Hockey Term (page 34)
1. penalty
2. referee
3. goaltender
4. defensemen
5. body check
6. champion
7. misconduct
8. equipment
9. tournament
10. Canada
11. breakaway
12. enforcer
13. overtime
14. power play
15. stick-handling

Skating Headlines (page 35)
1. Hayes Jenkins, David Jenkins
2. Jayne Torville, Christopher Dean
3. Oksana Baiul
4. Dorothy Hamill
5. Sonja Henie
6. Scott Hamilton
7. David Peletier, Jamie Sale
8. Tara Lipinski
9. Richard Button
10. Sergei Grinko
11. Todd Eldredge
12. Sura Bonaly
13. Michelle Kwan
14. Ilia Kulik
15. Midori Ito

Soccer

Names 'n' Numbers (page 36)
Names
1. Edson Arantes do Nascimento (also known as Pele)
2. San Siro
3. Luis Suarez
4. Diego Maradona
5. Peter Shilton
6. World Cup
7. Maracana Stadium, Rio de Janeiro, Brazil
8. Santos
Numbers
1. 11
2. 4
3. 4
4. 2
5. 1
6. 90
7. 45
8. 15
9. 100–130
10. 50–100
11. 24
12. 8

The World's Best (page 37)
This soccer player was born in **Brazil**. At age 15, he played for the **Santos**, a professional soccer club. He was a talented **forward** and led his team to three **world** championships. He **retired** in 1973, but in 1975, he returned to play for the New York **Cosmos**.
The full name of the world's best soccer player is **Edson Arantes do Nascimento**, but he is best known by his nickname, **Pele**.

Soccer Positions and Skills (page 38)

Tournament Trivia (page 39)
1. World Cup, 1994
2. World Cup, 1982
3. World Cup, 1990
4. World Cup, 1970
5. World Cup, 1958
6. World Cup, 1994
7. Olympics, 1996
8. World Cup, 1986
9. World Cup, 1994
10. Olympics, 1996
11. World Cup, 1991
12. Olympics, 1992
Bonus: World Cup, 1991; Olympics, 1996

You Be the Official (page 40)

1. Caution or Expulsion

2. Advantage

3. Direct Free Kick

4. Indirect Free Kick

5. Penalty Kick

6. Throw-in

7. Goal Kick

8. Substitution

Swimming and Diving

Swimming Words (page 41)
1. beach
2. goggles
3. swim
4. sink
5. cap
6. wave
7. sand
8. dive
9. race
10. kick
11. flip
12. water
13. flipper
14. float
15. laps
16. trunks
17. pool

Answer Key

Swimming Medalists (page 42)
1. Mark Spitz
2. Matt Biondi
3. Gary Hall, Jr.
4. Tom Jager
5. Don Schollander
6. Johnny Weissmuller
7. Jenny Thompson
8. Dara Torres
9. Shirley Babashoff
10. Amy Van Dyken
11. Angel Martino
12. Janet Evans

Bonus: Buster Crabbe and Johnny Weismuller

Swimming Glossary (page 43)
1. dive
2. platform
3. lanes
4. goggles
5. crawl
6. butterfly
7. relay
8. official
9. synchronize
10. tuck
11. pike
12. cramp
13. flutter
14. shallow
15. coach

Letter Puzzles (page 44)
1. swimming + diving
2. rivers, lakes, seas
3. tuck, pike, straight
4. Spitz, Evans, Biondi
5. synchronized swimming
6. springboard + platform
7. bathing suit, goggles
8. speed and stamina
9. Never swim alone.

Take the Plunge! (page 45–47)
Straight

Pike

Tuck

Tennis

Tennis Categories (page 48)
1. scoring terms
2. racket parts
3. shoe parts
4. equipment
5. strokes
6. tournaments
7. court surfaces
8. court areas
9. pro men players
10. pro women players

Tennis Doubles (page 49)
I. Andre Agassi, Arthur Ashe, Boris Becker, Bjorn Borg
II. Jennifer Capriati, Steffi Graf, Todd Martin, Billie Jean King
III. Jan Michael Gambill, Andy Roddick, Joseph Sirianni
IV. Bobby Riggs, Jimmy Connors
V. Pete Sampras, Monica Seles, Rennae Stubbs

Bonus: Venus and Serena Williams

Tennis Glossary (page 50)
1. ace
2. advantage
3. baseline
4. deuce
5. fault
6. forehand
7. game point
8. lob
9. love
10. match
11. net
12. rally
13. serve
14. set
15. volley

10 "S" Stars (page 51)
Part A:
1. Pete Sampras, United States
2. Serena Williams, United States
3. Monica Seles, Yugoslavia
4. Steffi Graf, West Germany
5. Stefan Edberg, Sweden
6. Sebastien Lareau, Canada
7. Gabriela Sabatini, Argentina
8. Rennae Stubbs, Australia
9. Stan Smith, United States
10. Manuel Santana, Spain

Part B:
1. Australian Open
2. French Open
3. British Open (Wimbledon)
4. U.S. Open

Part C:
1. Steffi Graf
2. Rod Laver
3. Martina Navratilova
4. William Renshaw

Tennis "Term-inator" (page 52)
Part A:
1. net
2. love
3. ball
4. block
5. ace
6. shot
7. volley
8. let ball
9. stroke

Part B:
1. lob
2. coach
3. racket
4. match
5. serve
6. grip
7. singles
8. handle
9. set or net

What a Racket! (page 53)

Part A:

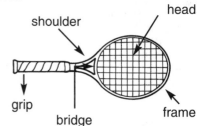

Part B:
1. badminton
2. table tennis
3. racquetball
4. squash

Tennis "Virtual" Point (page 54)

Diagram:

(diagram showing tennis court with baseline, net, singles sideline, service line, Joe, Shawn)

Play Plan: Answers will vary.

Track and Field

Word Within Words (page 55)
1. let
2. hot
3. on
4. cat
5. is, us
6. vent
7. rip
8. am, ring
9. king
10. print
11. ear
12. eat
13. rat, on
14. ill
15. ton

Answer Key

You've Got Mail (page 56)
Answers will vary.

How Do You Measure Up? (page 57)
Part A:
1. 624 feet
2. 325 feet
3. 358 feet
4. 195 feet
5. 4875 feet, 5280 feet, 405 feet

Part B:
1. 61.54 meters
2. 6.15 meters
3. 650.00 feet
4. 23.33 meters
5. 8.59 meters
6. 69.97 meters
7. 8.9 meters

Track-and-Field Events (page 58)
Part A:
1. sprint
2. middle distance
3. stadion
4. relay
5. high jump
6. hurdles
7. steeplechase
8. marathon
9. triple jump
10. pole vault
11. shot-put
12. discus
13. javelin
14. heptathlon
15. decathlon

Bonus: athletics

Volleyball
Volleyball Rules (page 59)
1. William
2. court
3. net
4. six
5. two
6. six
7. clockwise
8. ball
9. three
10. hands
11. receive a foul
12. side out
13. match
14. 15
15. two

Oops, It's All My Fault! (page 60)
1,2,3,9,10 are volleyball faults, 25 points (non-deciding game) 15 points (deciding game)

Volleyball Glossary (page 61)
1. match
2. rally
3. kill
4. court
5. spike
6. attacker
7. fault
8. sanction
9. referee
10. substitute
11. beach
12. kneepads
13. rotation
14. leather
15. mintonette

General Section
Team Sports Stars Anagrams (page 62)
Baseball
1. Roberto Alomar
2. Barry Larkin
3. Derek Jeter
4. Sammy Sosa
5. Cal Ripken, Jr.

Basketball
1. Patrick Ewing
2. Vince Carter
3. Shaquille O'Neal
4. Scottie Pippen
5. Karl Malone

Football
1. Johnny Unitas
2. John Elway
3. Dan Marino
4. Deion Sanders
5. Terrell Davis

Team-Sports Analogies (page 63)
1. football
2. catcher
3. referee
4. helmet
5. golf
6. puck
7. blades
8. head coach
9. six
10. hand
11. soccer
12. football

Bonus:
1. basketball, baseball
2. court, field
3. Lions, baseball, basketball

Individual-Sports Analogies (page 64)
1. throwing
2. diving
3. running
4. skiing
5. distance
6. club
7. court
8. archery
9. 6
10. shoot
11. pedal
12. head

Bonus:
1. golf, tennis
2. ball, disk
3. wrestling, skiing

Awesome American Athletes from the Past (page 65)
1. 100 points; March 2, 1962
2. pitcher; 27 seasons
3. figure skater; first American Olympic gold medal
4. running back; 99-yard touchdown
5. golfer; oldest to win Masters title
6. gymnast; all-around Olympic gold medal
7. center; all-time leading NHL scorer
8. swimmer; 7 Olympic gold medals
9. 1975; Wimbledon
10. boxer; Athlete of the Century

Sort the Pros (page 66)
NHL: Rangers, Red Wings, Bruins
NFL: 49ers, Cowboys, Bills
NBA: Bulls, Lakers, Celtics
MLB: Reds, Mariners, Yankees

Identifying Unusual Sports (page 67)
1. broomball
2. cricket
3. croquet
4. cycling
5. fencing
6. karate
7. lacrosse
8. luge
9. polo
10. rugby
11. squash
12. table tennis

Name the Pro Teams (page 68)
Part A:
1. Giants
2. Warriors
3. Saints
4. Cowboys
5. Yankees
6. Kings
7. Suns
8. Heat
9. Bulls
10. Wild

Part B:
1. Rangers
2. Twins
3. Cubs
4. Colts
5. Jets
6. Rams
7. Browns
8. Rockets
9. Clippers
10. Hornets

Sports Categories (page 69)
1. quarterback, baseball
2. home run, basketball
3. singlet, boxing
4. Frisbee, figure skating
5. toe pick, football
6. racket, golf
7. umpire, gymnastics
8. ball, ice hockey

Answer Key

9. puck, skiing
10. service line, soccer
11. pike, swimming
12. squash, tennis
13. stroke, track
14. dive, weightlifting
15. club, archery

Categorically Speaking (page 70)

1. television
2. clock
3. car
4. basket
5. football
6. announcer
7. neck
8. foot
9. skipping
10. hurdles
11. cycling
12. archery
13. marathon
14. skating
15. spectator

Early Names of Common Games
(page 71)

1. hockey
2. table tennis
3. tennis
4. golf
5. lacrosse
6. basketball
7. racquetball
8. croquet
9. cricket
10. baseball
11. shuffleboard
12. badminton
13. handball
14. soccer
15. volleyball

Plates of the Pros (page 72)
Answers will vary.
Bonus: Answers will vary.
Points of Origin (page 73)

1. France
2. England
3. Canada
4. U.S.
5. U.S.
6. Scotland
7. Norway
8. Switzerland
9. Japan
10. Greece
11. France
12. France
13. England
14. Spain
15. England

Winning Women (page 74)

1. tennis
2. figure skating; O
3. soccer; O
4. golf
5. tennis
6. swimming; O
7. track; O
8. gymnastics; O
9. track and field; O
10. soccer; O
11. marathon; O
12. volleyball; O
13. swimming; O
14. speed skating; O
15. skiing; O

Bonus: $1 + 5 - 4 = 2$

Sports Web Sites

Baseball

Yahoo! MLB Players site listings

Yahoo! MLB Team Pages

http://cbs.sportsline.com/u/fans/celebrity/ripken/2131/lou.html

http://baseball-almanac.com

Basketball

Yahoo! NBA Players site listings shows Abdul-Jabbar (w/ hyphen)

www.nba.com also has Abdul-Jabbar (w/ hyphen)

Football

Yahoo! NFL Players site listings

http://www.firstbasesports.com/handsig/football/ftbhsi.htm (hand signals)

Gymnastics

http://members.aol.com/msdaizy/sports3/gloss7.html

Skating and Hockey

http://members.aol.com/msdaizy/sports/gloss4.html

Yahoo! Skaters site listings (men and women)

Soccer

http://cbc.ca/olympics/02_sports/20_soccer/soccer_rules.html

http://www.360soccer.com/pele/pelebio.html (Pele)

http://www.firstbasesports.com/handsig/soccer/scrhsi.htm (hand signals)

Swimming and Diving

http://www.factmonster.com/ipka/A0115090.html (medalists)

http://members.aol.com/msdaizy/sports/bassw.html

Tennis

http://www.gottennis.com/pages/dictionary.htm

Yahoo! Tennis Players site listings (women and men)

Volleyball

http://www.volleyball.org/

General

http://www.myteam.com/ (Choose a sport.)

http://tsn.sportingnews.com